Low-Single-Deckers

GAVIN BOOTH

KEY
Books

BRITAIN'S BUSES SERIES, VOLUME 14

Front cover image: Over the past 30 years, low-floor single-deckers have become the norm in the UK. This is a 2002 Volvo B7L with Wright Eclipse Metro 41-seat body, photographed against the backdrop of York City Walls and Minster in 2007.

Back cover image: Representing the latest breed of single-deckers in the UK, this is a 2018 BYD D8UR with Alexander Dennis 31-seat body from RATP's London United fleet, at Victoria in 2021.

Title page image: Looking suitably long and low, a 1999 Dennis Dart SLF with Marshall 38-seat body is in Liverpool in 2012. Its interior layout is typical of most UK deliveries, with a low-entry rather than totally low-floor and raised seating towards the rear.

Contents page image: Although most low-floor buses have been diesel-powered, manufacturers and operators have moved away to zero-emission models like this 37-seat battery-electric Yutong E12 of McGill's, seen in Glasgow in 2022.

Acknowledgements
I am grateful to Keith McGillivray, Robert McGillivray, Sholto Thomas and Richard Walter for providing images that fill gaps in my own collection. Their photographs are credited throughout the book; all uncredited photos are my own.

Published by Key Books
An imprint of Key Publishing Ltd
PO Box 100
Stamford
Lincs PE19 1XQ

www.keypublishing.com

The right of Gavin Booth to be identified as the author of this book has been asserted in accordance with the Copyright, Designs and Patents Act 1988 Sections 77 and 78.

Contents

Chapter 1

The Move Away from High-Floor Buses

There are some 40,000 low-floor single-deckers in use in the UK – and counting. It took the bus industry the best part of the 20th century to acknowledge that the Latin word 'omnibus' really does mean *for all*. Not just the people in the community who were fit enough to clamber up a few steps to start their bus journey, but those with visible and invisible disabilities who found using buses difficult and often impossible. For people in wheelchairs, there were specially adapted buses and coaches that could accommodate them, but these denied users the advantages of using regular timetabled buses that allowed them to travel where and when they wanted. It was the same for parents with buggies and pushchairs, who often had to fold these up and suffer the indignity and inconvenience of boarding buses with a child under one arm and a pushchair under the other.

When I was involved with the Bus Users organisation, we regularly met people who could not travel by bus as often as they wished because of the difficulties they faced. Even when the first low-floor buses took to the streets of the UK in the mid-1990s, they were still in the minority, and there was no guarantee that the bus that turned up would be a new low-floor model or an older step-entrance one.

Gradually, the situation eased, helped in no small way by the Disabled Persons Transport Advisory Committee (DPTAC), which ensured that, from 31 December 2000, all new buses on local services had to be suitable for all passengers, and that included wheelchair users. Low-floor types had increasingly featured in orders for new single-deckers since 1993, and it became inevitable that double-deckers had to follow suit. The first UK low-floor double-decker went into service in February 1998.

The low-floor double-decker has been covered in the companion book to this, published by Key Books in 2021, and this book follows a similar pattern, concentrating, where possible in the text and the photographs, on single-deckers with their original owners and in original liveries. As there have been more single-deck than double-deck models, we cover the diesel-engined models by manufacturer in two bites – first the early models, and then the later models that were often better tailored to UK requirements, and to increasingly stringent European emissions standards. We will then look at the gas, hybrid diesel-electric, pure electric and hydrogen models that are becoming increasingly familiar on our streets, often from companies that are new to the bus-building market, which in turn has prompted the longer-established builders to develop their own non-diesel ranges or collaborate with the growing list of new entrants with experience in battery production.

Two of the earliest low-floor single-deckers, Dennis Lance SLFs with Wright Pathfinder 320 bodies, were shown to bus operators around the UK in March 1994. On the left is one of a batch of ten that had been introduced on to London route 120 in January that year, alongside a new Coastline bus, from Northern General's Tynemouth & District fleet.

When early low-floor single-deckers were in service, the manufacturers issued photos showing how easy it was to get buggies on and off this new breed of bus. This is a Brighton Blue Bus Dennis Dart SLF with 39-seat Plaxton Pointer body when new in 1996. Operators trumpeted the advantages of these new easy-access buses, although from the front, this bus merely has a graphic of a child in a pushchair; on the cantrail panel above the side windows, though, it lists some of the passengers who would benefit: 'kiddies in buggies, shoppers with trolleys, commuters in a hurry... the bus for everybody'. (Dennis)

Above: Another manufacturer's image, showing how easy it was for passengers with a buggy to board this 1996 Plymouth Citybus 39-seat Dennis Dart SLF/Plaxton Pointer, branded SuperRider, with a prominent arrow indicating how low the floor level was, a device also used by other operators. (Dennis)

Left: This is what low-floor single-deckers replaced in some areas – high-floor underfloor-engined buses with a steep and awkwardly-positioned step up to the driver and another for passengers to trip over after they had paid their fare. This is a 1979 Seddon Pennine 7/Alexander AYS type in the Midland Scottish fleet. (Sholto Thomas)

Operators and manufacturers were moving towards making it easier for passengers to board their buses. On step-entrance types like the Dennis Lance, this could involve a split-step arrangement with a lower section to the right, as on these two 1994 Lances with Alexander 39-seat PS type bodies undergoing final preparation at the Alexander coachworks at Falkirk before delivery to the Selkent fleet in London. The white band above the grey skirt roughly equates to the promisingly low floor level. Passengers boarding on the left had one further step to the interior, while those on the right had two shallower steps to negotiate.

Nearly 30 years after the first low-floor single-deckers took to the UK streets, the breed had been refined in ways that would not have been believed in 1993, with operators moving away from diesel engines towards zero emissions. Wright, which had played a major part in pioneering low-floor single-deckers, showed its hydrogen-powered Hydroliner GB Kite model at the ITT Hub event at Farnborough in 2022, claiming 'the ability to refuel' in less than 10 mins and a range of over 650 miles. (Keith McGillivray)

Chapter 2

The Long Road to Low-Floor

For many years, bus builders and bus operators seemed to give little thought to the needs of older or less-able passengers. Until the early 1970s, most buses consisted of a chassis built at A and a body built at B, often hundreds of miles apart and sometimes hundreds of miles from the operator's home patch.

The chassis builders offered a catalogue of models, and operators chose the combination of engines, gearboxes and brakes that best suited the requirements of the engineers. The bodybuilders offered standard designs that could be tweaked for more important customers in terms of the number and type of seats, the provision of a second door – and in broad terms, that was it. The aim was often to fit as many seats as legally possible into the body structure, and little thought seemed to be given to the needs of passengers who had difficulty using buses because of infirmity, disability or simply old age. For the traffic people and the bean-counters, getting as many passengers as possible into a single bus seemed to make sense.

There had been brave attempts to make boarding easier for passengers in the 1930s – Gilford's front-wheel drive double-decker in 1931 and Leyland's Low-Floor Trolley Bus in 1935 – but these remained one-off prototypes. The Bristol/Eastern Coach Works Lodekka, first introduced in 1949, provided stepless access for lower deck passengers, mainly to offer a low-height bus with normal seating on both decks. This was a hugely successful type, and in its 14-year production run, over 5,200 were built for state-owned Tilling and Scottish Bus fleets. But while these made life easier for many passengers, they still could not accommodate pushchairs or wheelchairs.

Things got better for less-able passengers from the 1960s, when the first rear-engined double-deckers were entering service in increasing numbers. These had wider doors and were easier for passengers to board, with few if any additional steps to negotiate to access the lower deck. When the first rear-engined single-deckers followed during the 1960s, the easier entrances and lower floor levels (made possible by mounting the engine right at the back) were in stark contrast to the previous generation of underfloor-engined types that had, of necessity, several steps at the entrance and a high floor level. Many examples of this new breed had a single, often shallow, step up from the front platform to the gangway

Not that the appearance of rear-engined single-deckers heralded the end of the underfloor-engined models with their steep entrance steps, as some operators continued to buy these into the 1980s. And not just the conservative ones like the Scottish Bus Group companies. The emerging giant Stagecoach, which could never be described as conservative, had a need to buy large quantities of new buses to top up and modernise the fleets of the companies it had picked up on its seemingly relentless acquisition trail. It chose the mid-engined Volvo B10M coupled to an Alexander PS type body and went on to buy more than 600 of these between 1992 and 1998. Although mid-engined, these buses had a commendably low floorline and bought Stagecoach some valuable time while it was considering which of the new low-floor single-deckers best suited its needs.

South Yorkshire PTE also went down the B10M/PS route, but most operators opted for the new breed of rear-engined single-decker. The first generation of these had appeared in the 1960s, built by manufacturers that found themselves swept up into the conglomerate that became British Leyland. Good, and not so good, chassis from AEC, Albion, Bristol, Daimler and Leyland were sacrificed at the altar of the Leyland National, a highly-standardised new model that resulted from a partnership between Leyland and the National Bus Company (NBC).

There were operators who were not convinced that the National was the answer to their dreams, and those who resented Leyland's dominant position and its apparent take-it-or-leave-it approach. Metro-Cammell, which had been heavily involved in bodying single-deck buses for London Transport in the 1960s, recognised the threat to its business and teamed up with the Swedish manufacturer Scania to produce the Metro-Scania in 1969, based on an existing Scania model but bodied in Britain. Seddon, which was mainly a truck builder, was persuaded to produce a full-size bus chassis in 1969 with a rear-mounted Gardner engine, aimed at operators that were mourning the absence of the much-loved Bristol RELL. In 1973, Seddon also created a mid-engined chassis, at the behest of the Scottish Bus Group, the Seddon Pennine 7, again with a Gardner engine.

What was probably the most significant new entrant to the British bus and coach market was the Swedish giant Volvo, which started selling its mid-engined B58 chassis in the UK from 1972. Most B58s were bodied as coaches, but its successor, the B10M, enjoyed great success between 1980 and 2002, including many with bus bodies, as we have seen, and even with double-deck bodies. The appearance of the B10M prompted Leyland to replace its popular (but ageing) Leopard with its new mid-engined Tiger chassis. Like the B10M, the Tiger mainly carried coach bodies, but it proved to be popular for bus work as well.

But preferences were changing. In the early 1980s, the Leyland National was facing increasing competition from new models from Dennis and Scania, and later in the decade from significant

The mass-produced Leyland National, a marriage of Leyland and the National Bus Company (NBC), was delivered, not surprisingly, to individual NBC companies, including some that would probably have preferred something else. This National 2 entered service with NBC's West Yorkshire company in 1981, and it is seen here in 1992 in Bradford, in service after privatisation with the Keighley & District company.

European players like DAF, Neoplan, Renault and Van Hool, with varying degrees of success. These were step-entrance rear-engined buses, although there were already stirrings on mainland Europe where Neoplan was pioneering low-floor designs.

There was also a growing interest in one-stop shopping. From the earliest days of motorbuses in the UK, there had been companies that built chassis and others that built bodies and operators were used to buying the main parts of their buses from two different, usually unrelated businesses. Firms like Crossley and Leyland could offer their customers complete buses, but their customers could still opt to have their chassis bodied elsewhere.

Leyland tried to buck this trend with the National city bus and its successor, the Lynx, which was assembled on a production line in Cumbria. But operators still continued to support their favoured suppliers, and new models appeared to cater for this market.

Fast forward to the 1990s, when the manufacturing industry was changing dramatically. Newcomers from mainland Europe like DAF, Mercedes-Benz, Scania and Volvo were competing with the diminishing band of UK bus builders and brought new ideas to the party. For some, it was persuading operators to buy complete vehicles, usually right-hand drive versions of their mainstream offerings.

For others, it was forming relationships with UK bodybuilders to offer certain exclusive chassis/body combinations.

And although fewer of the main players were now UK-based, there were important survivors that are still around today. Alexander and Dennis had survived the traumas of the Mayflower/TransBus years to bounce back as Alexander Dennis (AD) and recognised that complete AD buses were the way forward. Optare had started creating attractive models that initially involved Optare bodywork on proprietary chassis, but it gradually recognised the benefits of offering complete buses, notably the Excel in 1995 and the Solo in 1998. Wright had grown dramatically from its roots in Northern Ireland to become a major force on mainland Britain, first with bodies on chassis, then increasingly with its own range of complete buses.

Rear-engined single-deckers first became popular in the 1960s, and Bristol's RELL was the great survivor. While other Leyland models were withdrawn from the lists to stimulate sales for the new Leyland National, the step-entrance RELL was allowed to continue as an 'export' model for Ulsterbus and Citybus in Northern Ireland until 1982. This Citybus RELL6G with Alexander (Belfast) 39-seat X type body, seen in Belfast in 1996, was built in 1982 but only entered service in 1984.

Sales of full-size buses in the UK had slumped in the mid-1980s as operators faced the uncertainties of deregulation, which abandoned the strict licensing system of the previous 50 years, outside London, encouraging competition on the streets. A rash of new entrants took advantage of this new freedom, and while some succeeded, others quickly fell by the wayside or were bought over by the new groups that were emerging from the privatisation of the companies in the NBC and Scottish Bus Group, and subsequently the Passenger Transport Executives in the major conurbations and many former municipal companies.

Before the low-floor revolution hit the UK, there appeared an influx of new models that still had step entrances, but with lower and fewer steps, and which represented the first stage towards the introduction, acceptance and eventual domination of the low-floor layout.

Right: Leyland's response to the successful Volvo B10M was the mid-engined Tiger chassis, popular for bus and coach duties. In Colchester in 1990 is a 1982 Hedingham & District Tiger with step-entrance Plaxton Derwent 55-seat body.

Below: Scottish Bus Group companies invested heavily in mid-engined Leyland Leopards with high-floor Alexander Y type bodies. This 1982 Highland Scottish example, in Inverness in 1992, is a 62-seater, with rows of 3+2 seating towards the rear.

The mid-engined Volvo B10M chassis continued to be popular with some operators for some years after low-floor single-deckers first became available. Stagecoach was a loyal customer, buying more than 750 step-entrance B10M buses between 1992 and 1998, the majority with this style of Alexander PS type body. Although underfloor-engined, the floorline was commendably low. This 1997 Stagecoach example is in central Glasgow when new, alongside a competing example from First's Greater Glasgow fleet; both are 49-seaters.

In Northern Ireland, Translink built up a substantial fleet of Scania K230UBs with Wright Solar Rural 55-seat bodies between 2008 and 2011. This 2008 delivery is seen in Belfast in 2015. (Keith McGillivray)

Chapter 3

The Generation In-Between

Threw the Leyland National was imposed on many, sometimes reluctant fleets, and was bought by others in the absence of much choice or simply because buses were needed in a hurry. It prompted other manufacturers to enter the fray with competitive models, though sales were usually low compared with the mass-produced National.

A new breed of rear-engined single-decker started to appear in the 1980s. Dennis offered the Falcon from 1980 and the midi-sized Domino from 1985, but its greatest contribution to the UK bus industry was undoubtedly the Dart, which first appeared in step-entrance form in 1988. Leyland had replaced the National with the Lynx in 1985 after building over 7,000 Nationals, though the timing was not ideal as it coincided with an operating industry that was in turmoil as it faced the uncertainties of deregulation.

Operators released from subtle pressure to buy home market buses were attracted by new models coming from mainland Europe and had a growing list of models to choose from. DAF, based in the Netherlands, appeared on the UK scene with its SB220 chassis and went on to develop a range aimed at UK buyers. The French manufacturer Renault dabbled in the UK market without much success. Scania made a slow start with models from its K, L and N ranges, but blossomed in the 1990s with its low-floor chassis. But it was the other Swedish giant, Volvo, that would have the greatest impact on the UK market with successive models that have usually found widespread approval.

Back in the UK, there were new names nibbling at the single-deck bus market, notably Optare, which had taken over Leyland's former Roe coachworks in Leeds in 1985 and had quickly moved on from being purely a bodybuilder to develop a new range of models that initially used chassis from various builders, before moving on to concentrate on producing an attractive range of complete vehicles.

After Optare's first joint venture with DAF to produce the Optare Delta in 1988 (a full-size single-decker on DAF's SB220 chassis), there followed the midi-size Vecta on the MAN 11.180 in 1991, the full-size lightweight Sigma on the Dennis Lance in 1994, and the Prisma on the Mercedes-Benz O405 the following year.

Volvo cemented its UK presence in 1988 when it acquired the once-mighty Leyland Bus, which had been weakened by the difficult British Leyland years when managers had to balance the successful Leyland bus and truck range with the problems of the ailing British car industry. This hastened the demise of most Leyland models that duplicated Volvo's own range, except for the double-deck Olympian that, in a Volvo-ised version, continued to outsell its competition until 1997, and the Lynx that earned a brief reprieve until it was replaced by Volvo's B10B.

Operators had a growing choice of full-size step-entrance rear-engined single-deckers in the early 1990s. There was the DAF/Optare Delta; Dennis with its Falcon and Lance models; Scania with differently configured chassis from its K, L and N ranges; and Volvo had its B10B, the replacement for Leyland's Lynx. And these would be joined in 1992 by Mercedes-Benz, offering right-hand drive versions of its internationally popular O405 range.

The Optare models were marketed as complete vehicles, but the others received bodies built in the UK. With Leyland's family of bodybuilders out of the way, there were opportunities for long-established firms as well as newcomers that identified an opportunity to grow.

Alexander had broadened its horizons well beyond its Scottish base in the 1950s and was supplying bodies to operators in many parts of the world. Duple, primarily a builder of coach bodies, was building bus bodies on mid-engined chassis. East Lancashire Coachbuilders, known more commonly as East Lancs, had broadened its customer and product base beyond its traditional output of municipal double-deckers. Marshall had been active in the single-deck market in the 1950s and 1960s and bounced back in 1992 when it acquired the Carlyle business. Northern Counties, like East Lancs, had majored on double-deckers but responded to a demand for single-deckers in the 1990s. Plaxton was similar to its arch rival, Duple, building single-deck bus bodies in its quieter summer months.

And then there was Wright, based in Ballymena and well-established in its native Northern Ireland. It spread its wings in the 1990s with a range of attractive models; in the step-entrance era, there were Endurance bodies on Mercedes-Benz O405, Scania N113 and Volvo B10B chassis. Wright went from strength to strength later in the 1990s with a range of pioneering low-floor bodies, which bore a confusing selection of names, depending on the chassis these were mounted on.

Probably the most important step-entrance single-deck model of the time was not one of the full-length types, but a bus that grew from a recognition at Dennis that operators wanted something smaller than an 11–12m long single-decker but more substantial than the van-derived minibuses that had prospered briefly in the mid-1980s. The result was the Dart, the most popular bus chassis on the UK market from its introduction in 1988 as a joint venture between Dennis and Duple, both then stablemates in the Hestair Group. The Dart was subsequently reworked as a highly successful low-floor chassis and under Alexander Dennis morphed into the Enviro200 model.

The success of the Dart prompted Volvo to introduce the B6 model in 1992, which again developed into a low-floor chassis. DAF Bus introduced its Dart competitor, the SB120, in 2000, and this was low-floor from the start. The Dart and B6 offered a range of lengths between 8.5m and 9.9m, and as a low-floor bus the Dart grew to 11.3m. There was competition in the midi market from the Optare MetroRider, developed from the 1986 MCW Metrorider after MCW's closure, and while the Optare version sold well, its low-floor successor, the Solo, went on to greater things.

This posed 1994 Scania publicity shot features an L113CRL FlexCi with 49-seat step-entrance CountyBus Paladin bodywork by Northern Counties; the L113CRL would soon be available for low-floor bodies. Scania regularly contrived to obtain registration marks that echoed its chassis type designation. (Scania)

Leyland replaced the National with the Lynx in 1985, but uncertainty among operators following bus service deregulation in Britain outside London meant that sales were disappointing. Just over 1,000 Lynxes were built compared with over 7,700 Nationals. London operators bought few Lynxes – this 1989 Mk1 is at Richmond with London United.

The Optare Delta was a stylish full-size single-deck bus on a DAF SB220 chassis, and some 180 step-entrance SB220s were supplied to UK operators between 1988 and 1991, the majority with Optare bodies. This is a 1991 Delta delivery to Dennis's of Dukinfield, in Manchester in 1992.

The step-entrance Dennis Dart was initially developed by Dennis and Duple, which at the time were both part of the Hestair Group, and early Darts carried this style of Dartline body, which was subsequently built by Carlyle. The Dart would go on to be by far the most popular chassis of recent years, in its original and subsequent low-floor form. Although it carries Carlyle badging, this Southampton Citybus 1990 example is actually the third production Dart, and it has Duple Dartline 35-seat bodywork.

Introduced in 1990, the Leyland Lynx II had a more rounded front end, but any sales potential was short-lived after Volvo acquired Leyland Bus in 1988 and decided to replace it with its own B10B model. This Lothian Buses example, at its launch at Edinburgh Castle in 1991, was one of the only batch of Lynxes built to two-door layout, other than Leyland prototypes and a single bus exported to Singapore.

The Dennis Dart was available in different chassis lengths; this 1992 London United 8.5m Dart with Plaxton Pointer 24-seat body is at London Heathrow Airport in 2002.

The Dennis Lance was a lightweight step-entrance 11.5m chassis, essentially a larger Dart, and some 400 were delivered to UK operators. This is the third Lance built, as a Dennis demonstrator in 1992. It has a 47-seat Plaxton Verde 47-seat body and is seen in Dundee in 1994 after sale to Tayside.

The 1993 Arriva Yorkshire Dennis Lance has a 47-seat Alexander Strider AF type body, and the 1996 First Leeds example alongside it has a Plaxton Verde 49-seat body. They are seen in Leeds in 2001.

The B6 was Volvo's slightly belated reaction to the midi-size Dennis Dart, but sales of over 600 chassis never came near to matching the Dart's runaway success. This is a GM Buses North 1994 B6 with Northern Counties Paladin 40-seat bodywork, in Manchester in 1991. Vinyls on the side windows draw attention to its green engine, air suspension and low steps.

Volvo replaced the Lynx that it had inherited with the acquisition of Leyland Bus in 1988 with its B10B chassis and went on to sell 580 to UK operators between 1993 and 1997, like this 1995 GM Buses North 'Superbus' delivery with Wright Endurance 50-seat body. Although true low-floor buses were starting to appear in the UK, this bus still boasted a 'low floor', even though it was reached by a two-step entrance – as well as double-glazing, luxury seating, air suspension and a green engine.

Right: This Volvo B10B with Plaxton Verde two-door 45-seat body, seen in 2003, was delivered to the Oxford Bus Company in 1997.

Below: Optare raised the minibus stakes with its step-entrance MetroRider model, which had started life as the MCW Metrorider; when MCW pulled out of bus building, Optare bought the rights and re-engineered it – its first move into building complete vehicles. This 2003, 8.5m-long MetroRider 29-seater is in Grassington in 2004, working for Pride of the Dales.

Chapter 4

The Operators

Following the upheavals of the 1980s, with bus service deregulation and the privatisation of the NBC the future shape of the UK bus industry was beginning to evolve in the early 1990s. By the end of that decade, the privatisation of the Scottish Bus Group companies and the PTE bus operations – and the subsequent acquisitions and mergers – had created a smaller number of major players, each with its own vehicle-buying policy. The main groups were Arriva, FirstGroup, Go-Ahead and Stagecoach, which today operate a combined total of some 23,000 buses in the UK. Other significant groups include Comfort DelGro, National Express West Midlands, RATP Dev, and Translink in Northern Ireland, each operating over 1,000 buses. Last but not least, there are Lothian, Rotala, Transdev and Wellglade, each with fleets of more than 500 buses.

Where once there had been nearly 100 municipal operators in the UK, the creation of PTEs and the subsequent privatisation frenzy has reduced the number of survivors to single figures. However, of these, Lothian and Nottingham have the greatest clout when buying new buses, with Lothian recently investing in 98 new diesel double-deckers and Nottingham amassing a fleet of over 100 biogas double-deckers.

So, with a total of some 30,000 buses between them, these operators have the greatest buying power and work with chassis and bodybuilders to get the buses that best suit their operating territories and their engineers. And with the biggest groups placing substantial orders each year, the groups have often had to shop around to ensure timeous deliveries, which means that strict standardisation has often had to be abandoned in the interests of keeping fleets up to date.

Of the four largest groups, Arriva has bought a range of types from the major suppliers, often to suit the needs of its operating companies, but when it could it supported its sister company, Arriva Bus & Coach, which sold DAF/VDL models into the UK, and has turned to Scania and Volvo for heavier chassis.

FirstGroup orders had helped the growth of the Wright business, which had become an important supplier in Britain as well as its native Northern Ireland, and First bought many hundreds of Wright bodies on Scania and Volvo low-floor single-deck chassis, and also became a major customer for the Wright StreetLite in varying lengths. The Go-Ahead Group has also shopped around, with most of the major diesel models represented in its fleets, as well as Chinese-built BYD (Build Your Dreams) and Yutong electrics.

Stagecoach was initially cautious when low-floor single-deck models became available. It bought Dennis Darts and Optare Solos for its midi-size fleet, but stuck to the mid-engined step-entrance Volvo B10M until 1998 and soon turned to the MAN/Alexander combination for its full-size low-floor duties.

Analysis of the low-floor single-deckers that all the groups have bought shows that they all shopped around when they had to and had accumulated rather mixed fleets by 2010, after which they faced the new future with choices between hybrid, electric, biogas and hydrogen buses.

Arriva Bus & Coach, importing DAF and later VDL chassis to the UK, was inevitably looking to its sister operating companies to buy lots of its chassis, which of course they did, but the demand for new buses and coaches was such that Arriva, like the other major groups, had to shop around for new vehicles. So, in addition to substantial deliveries of DAF and VDL models – like this DAF SB120 with Wright Cadet 39-seat bodywork, new in 2002 to Arriva Midlands and seen in Shrewsbury in 2006 – Arriva has bought ADL, MAN, Mercedes-Benz, Optare, Scania, Volvo and Wright products.

FirstGroup's roots are in the former GRT Group, based in Aberdeen, and the local fleet is often used to trial new types, like this 2005 Volvo B7LA with 56-seat Wright Eclipse Fusion body, seen in 2008. At an early stage, First cultivated a relationship with Wright, which had previously been a smaller coachbuilder supplying its native Northern Ireland market. First has bought large quantities of Wright bodies on single-deck and double-deck chassis, often Volvos, but has also bought from other UK and European manufacturers to keep its fleet age profile up to date.

Scottish-based Stagecoach has tended to support Alexander for its bodywork needs and, more recently, Alexander Dennis for complete vehicles. The group has bought from most of the major players, and for its first bulk low-floor orders it turned to MAN, and the MAN 18 series with Alexander ALX300 42-seat bodywork became a staple in many of its UK fleets. This is a 1999 18.220 delivery to the Stagecoach Fife Buses fleet.

The Go-Ahead Group has its roots in the Northern General company in north-east England, but it has expanded with group companies in various parts of England. In Newcastle, in 2001, is a 1999 Optare Excel 41-seater.

Although the main focus of the National Express bus business was on its West Midlands heartland, it expanded in 1997 when it acquired the Tayside business and branded it National Express Dundee. This 2010 Scania K230UB OmniLink 43-seater is seen in 2011, wearing the corporate livery of the time.

The Transdev Group operations stretch across northern England, from Preston to the Yorkshire Coast, with some 550 buses. This 2012 Harrogate & District Optare Versa 11.1m 36-seater is at Boroughbridge in 2017, branded for the Harrogate Connect services. (Robert McGillivray)

There are still areas dominated by larger independent companies, and McGill's has built up a substantial business in Glasgow and in the area west of the city. In Paisley, in 2017, is a 2007 Volvo B7RLE with 37-seat Wright Eclipse Urban body, acquired with Arriva's former Scotland West business in 2012.

The Wellglade Group has a significant presence in the East Midlands. This TrentBarton 2000 Optare Solo 9.2m 34-seater is at Hucknall station, providing a connecting service with the Nottingham Express Transit (NET) tram in 2007.

Chapter 5

The First Low-Floor Models

At first glance, manufacturers on mainland Europe had an advantage over UK-based companies. They had enthusiastically embraced low-floor single-deckers from the start and were investing in these. However, this was because of the very different financial regime, where bus operations in Europe were often shored up by high levels of subsidy. Expense seemed to be no object for many city fleets across much of Europe; in the UK, things were very different.

The first low-floor single-deckers that UK operators could examine on their home turf were brought over to Liverpool in September 1992 by Merseytravel, the local PTE: from the Netherlands, there was a Berkhof-bodied MAN NL202, and a Den Oudsten Alliance City; from Belgium, a Van Hool A300; and from Germany, a Neoplan N4014. These were left-hand drive buses with seats for as few as 24 passengers and standing space for as many as 69 more – not quite what UK operators were looking for, but still an opportunity to examine this new breed.

The trip to Liverpool was initially and briefly most beneficial for Neoplan, which had been building low-floor buses since the 1970s, and which won an order from Merseytravel. In May 1993, the first of these was the first low-floor single-decker to enter service in the UK, followed in September by a Scania/East Lancs MaxCi for Tayside. These were based on well-established chassis, but the first UK-built low-floor buses were Wright Pathfinder-bodied Dennis Lance SLFs for London United in January 1994, followed in London later in the year by similarly bodied Scania N113 MaxCis for the East London and Leaside operations.

Now there was a rush among manufacturers to get suitable low-floor chassis into the UK market. There was an acceptance that UK operators were looking for something simpler than the buses in service in mainland Europe. They had to be lighter, less complex and, yes, cheaper, and where many European types had low floors throughout, often in connection with a third door behind the rear axle (which could mean seats on pedestals), the UK market tended to favour low-*entry* buses. These had all the advantages of fully low-floor buses at the entrance and to a point just ahead of the rear axle, where steps led to a higher section towards the rear; this allowed passengers with wheelchairs or buggies to use the forward part of the saloon, while in theory more able passengers occupied the seats in the rear.

There were successes and failures, as we shall see, but in the 20 years following the first appearance on the streets of the UK of this new breed of bus, over 60 new models were introduced, built by 15 different manufacturers. Only five of these manufacturers were UK-based, most of the rest were from mainland Europe. A couple – Designline from New Zealand and King Long from China – came from countries in the Southern Hemisphere, and this was before the appearance of substantial deliveries of Chinese-built battery-electric buses in the 21st century. The bus supply business had become truly international, a far cry from the days when every new bus for the UK was built in the UK, and, in the 1970s, mostly by British Leyland. It was also a far cry from the time when manufacturers like AEC and Leyland generally fitted their own engines in their chassis, whereas others, including Bristol and Daimler, did offer their own engines, but their customers tended to go for the much-loved Gardner range.

Diesel-engined low-floor single-deckers from MAN, Mercedes-Benz, Scania and Volvo have always fitted their own engines, and MAN engines are also found in some Optare models. The DAF SB220 used a DAF engine, but its lighter SB120/180/200 chassis used Cummins engines, which had become very much the engine of choice for many of the Alexander Dennis, BMC, Dennis, Marshall, Plaxton and some Optare models described in this book.

Ever-stricter European emission standards for heavy-duty diesel engines have led to a constant need for engine manufacturers to upgrade their engines and their chassis to meet the changes. Starting with Euro I in 1992, over the following 20 years these regulations became increasingly stringent, with Euro VI coming into force at the end of 2012. Since that time, there has been a dramatic move away from diesel-powered engines with the advent of hybrid diesel-electric, biogas, battery electric and hydrogen models. These are covered in a later chapter.

We shall now look at the first wave of products by manufacturer, chronologically, based on their first deliveries to UK operators.

Neoplan

The German-based bus and coach builder, Neoplan, deserves its first place in this section. Its work developing the first low-floor buses in 1976 grew from its experience reducing front axle intrusion on its legendary double-deck coaches, which had to meet the strict 4m overall height restrictions in much of mainland Europe.

A left-hand drive version of Neoplan's N4014 was one of the four low-floor buses brought across to the UK in 1992 by Merseytravel and exhibited in Liverpool. This led to an order from Merseytravel for an N4014, and this bus went into service in May 1993, to be followed early in 1994 by 12 N4016 models. However, by this time other manufacturers had done a bit of catching up, and the 13 Neoplans were destined to be the only low-floor Neoplans bought for UK service. These 13 Neoplans were operated for Merseyside PTE by Arriva North West and Wales.

Seen in Liverpool in 2005, this is one of the 13 pioneering Merseyside PTE Neoplan N4016 33-seaters operated by Arriva.

Dennis

Two models marked the resurgence of Dennis as a major force in the bus industry – the Dominator double-deck chassis introduced in 1977 and the Dart, which had first appeared as a step-entrance chassis in 1988. Although the Dennis company had been around for most of the 20th century, building buses, trucks and fire engines for a select band of customers, these, the Dart in particular, propelled Dennis into the big league of bus builders. Dennis sold nearly 3,500 step-entrance Darts between 1988 and 1998, creating a family of midi-size buses, available in various lengths.

Dennis quickly recognised that there would be an increasing interest in low-floor single-deckers after the first examples appeared on Merseyside and responded to a call from London Buses for a seed batch of buses, to be bodied by Wright. The first of these took to the streets in January 1994 on Dennis Lance SLF chassis and helped to establish the concept of full-size chassis that were lighter and potentially cheaper to operate than the models coming in from mainland Europe, like the Scanias that also featured in those early London experiments. Just over 100 Lance SLFs were built, but they gave Dennis the experience with lightweight low-floor buses in service that led to the hugely successful Dart SLF.

The Dennis business survived changes of ownership in the 1970s and 1980s, first when it was acquired by the Hestair Group in 1972, then when the vehicle interests were bought out by a management team in 1988 as Trinity Holdings. But then Henlys, which already owned coachbuilders Plaxton, tried to buy Dennis. It was outbid by Mayflower, which had bought coachbuilders Alexander in 1995, and these businesses were grouped under the TransBus International name. Problems caused the collapse of Mayflower, and TransBus went into administration in 2004. Alexander and Dennis were bought by a group of Scottish investors and rebranded Alexander Dennis, bringing Plaxton into the fold in 2007. Alexander Dennis was sold to Canada-based New Flyer Industries in 2019.

Through this difficult period, Dennis continued to build Dart chassis – nearly 9,000 of them between 1996 and 2008. One new model was introduced, the full-size Enviro300 chassis, which survived in production until 2015, with more than 1,000 delivered.

London Buses produced this leaflet to herald the introduction into service of its very first low-floor buses in January 1994 – Dennis Lance SLFs with Wright Pathfinder 38-seat bodies.

Above: Dennis Lance SLFs were among the first low-floor buses to enter service in the UK. There were 38 Lances with 11.2m long Wright Pathfinder 34-seat bodies delivered to the management-owned London United, CentreWest and Metroline companies in 1994. This is a CentreWest bus leaving Uxbridge in 1994 surrounded by London buses of the time – a Mercedes-Benz/Alexander minibus, an MCW Metrobus and a Leyland National.

Left: London United was an early customer for the new Dennis Dart SLF and this 1996 delivery with Wright Crusader 32-seat body was posed outside the former tram shed at Fulwell depot in the company of a step-entrance 1990 Dart with Carlyle body from the Selkent fleet, presumably to illustrate how much the technology had advanced in just six years. (Dennis)

Stagecoach was a major customer for the Dart SLF, usually with Alexander or Plaxton bodies. This is a 1997 10.9m Dart with two-door Alexander ALX200 29-seat body at London's Liverpool Street station in 2001, liveried for the service to London City Airport.

In 1997, the independent Mackie's of Alloa bought this UVG UrbanStar-bodied 43-seat Dart.

This is a Dennis Super Pointer Dart (SPD) with Plaxton Pointer 41-seat 11.3m-long body, one of a batch of 31 ordered by the Mainline company but placed in service by First Mainline after the business was acquired in 1998. This one is in Sheffield when new.

Liveried for the 555 route linking Walton and Shepperton with London Heathrow airport, this is a 1999 London United Dart with two-door 27-seat Plaxton Pointer 2 10.7m body at Heathrow in 2001.

A Metrobus 1999 Dart with 10.2m Plaxton Pointer 31-seat two-door body at East Croydon station in 2005, with a 1998 Tramlink Bombardier Flexity Swift tram in the background. The Dart is on the T33 tramway feeder service.

This 2000 First Orpington Buses Dart with Marshall Capital 28-seat body is operating the tram feeder T31 route when new, wearing a livery based on the Tramlink fleet.

A 2000 Connex Dart with 8.9m Alexander ALX200 28-seat body passes through Brixton in 2003.

A 2000 Dart MPD/Plaxton Pointer 29-seater of Harte of Greenock climbs out of Greenock in 2003, declaring itself to be a 'Super low floor easy access bus for all'.

Another Greenock area operator, Slaemuir Coaches, and a 2000 Dart/Plaxton Pointer in Greenock bus station in 2003, in the company of minibuses from the same fleet.

Hackney Community Transport won its first contract from Transport for London in 1999 and bought new Darts with 10.5m Caetano Nimbus 26-seat bodies in 2001 for the 153 route. One is seen at Liverpool Street station in 2002.

This Marshall Capital-bodied Dart was new in 2002 to First Capital and passed to Go-Ahead London in 2013, when First withdrew from London operations. It is in Romford in 2016.

Lothian Buses invested in 42-seat SPD Pointer Darts in 2002–03. This 2002 example is seen in Leith in 2003.

Leaving the bus station at Newport, Isle of Wight, in 2013, is a Southern Vectis 37-seat Pointer Dart, new in 2004.

Stagecoach continued to buy hundreds of Pointer Darts until 2007, when it switched to the Dart's successor, the Alexander Dennis Enviro200 Dart. By the time this 38-seat Pointer Dart was delivered to Stagecoach in Inverness in 2005, the difficulties of the TransBus years were past, and the buses were produced under the Alexander Dennis name.

The Enviro300 (E300), a full-length lightweight low-floor single-decker, first appeared during the TransBus era and remained on the Alexander Dennis model lists for 13 years, selling over 1,000 chassis. Stagecoach bought the E300 for its operating companies, represented by this 2006 44-seater from its Hampshire Bus fleet in the green Winchester Park & Ride livery in 2008.

In the then-current Stagecoach livery at the base station of the Cairngorm Mountain Railway in 2016, a 2007 60-seat E300 from the Highland Country fleet.

A facelifted 2007 E300 44-seater in Stagecoach Gold livery in the centre of Dundee in 2012. This style of front end was shared with other contemporary Alexander Dennis models following the demise of TransBus. The original style had been developed by Plaxton when it came under TransBus ownership.

The fast-growing Scottish independent operator, West Coast Motors, bought this 52-seat E300 in 2008 for its local services around Oban, where it is seen when new.

In Inverness in 2014, a 2013 40-seat E300 for the Stagecoach Highland Country fleet.

Another Stagecoach E300, this time at the other end of Britain in 2013 – a 2013 46-seater from the East Kent fleet working on the Canterbury Park and Ride service.

Scania

The Swedish giant Scania has been active in the UK market since 1980, first with step-entrance single-deck and double-deck bus chassis and then with a range of rear-engined coach chassis. Like other bus builders on mainland Europe in the 1990s, Scania had an advantage over UK firms as it already had well-established low-floor models on its lists and quickly produced right-hand drive versions.

Scania N113s were some of the first low-floor single-deck types go enter service in the UK – an East Lancs-bodied MaxCi for Tayside in 1993 and a batch of N113 with Wright bodies for London Buses in 1994.

In the 1990s, Scania offered chassis to carry UK-built bodies as well as complete integral buses built in Poland as the OmniCity and OmniLink; the OmniCity was also available in articulated form.

Scania's type designations related to the position of the rear engine – 'K' for an inline engine, 'L' for an inline engine inclined 60 degrees to the left, and 'N' for a transverse engine inclined 60 degrees to the rear; then the size of the engine, 9 or 11 litres; next either a '3' or '4' to indicate 3 series or 4 series chassis; and and lastly two letters to distinguish whether the bus was an Urban Articulated (UA) or Urban Bus (UB) model. So, an L94UB was a 4 series Urban Bus chassis with a 9-litre inline/inclined engine, for bodying locally, and the CN94UB was similar with a transverse engine and Scania-built body – the initial 'C' indicating complete Scania buses.

Right: This early low-floor Scania L113CRL with Wright Axcess-ultralow 42-seat body, seen in Manchester in 1996, was new to Bullock of Cheadle in 1995, with vinyls indicating the low floorline and promoting easy access.

Below: A Translink 2003 L94UB with Wright Axcess Floline 43-seat body in Belfast in 2011.

A 2004 First Hampshire & Dorset OmniCity CN94UB 44-seater is at Fareham bus station in 2014, wearing the new style of corporate livery introduced by First in 2012.

On a wet 2008 day in Hereford, a Scania OmniCity CN94UB of DRM of Bromyard. It is a 2005 42-seater.

FirstGroup bought large batches of L94UBs with Wright Axcess Floline bodies. This First Scotland East 2005 example picks up passengers in Selkirk en route from Carlisle to Edinburgh in 2007.

This image shows a newly delivered 2006 N94UB OmniTown for Metrobus with East Lancs 29-seat two-door body, in Lewisham.

Volvo

In many ways, Volvo spearheaded the move by bus builders in mainland Europe into the UK market when it introduced a right-hand drive version of its popular mid-engined B58 chassis in 1972. The great majority of these were bodied as coaches, but when its successor, the B10M, came along in 1982, many received bus bodies, particularly for Stagecoach group fleets.

Volvo then set its sights on the rear-engined bus market in the UK. After it bought Leyland Bus in 1988, it continued to offer Leyland's Lynx, but in 1993 it introduced its step-entrance replacement, the B10B. But low-floor single-deckers were coming to the UK, and so there were a succession of Volvo models offered between 1994 and 2001: the full-sized B10L, B10BLE and B7L; the midi B6LE and B6BLE; and the articulated B10LA and B7LA. The B10BLE, with nearly 1,000 delivered, was the best seller of Volvo's initial offering, but at the same time Volvo was supplying thousands of its B7TL double-decker to UK and other markets. Volvo's type designations were relatively straightforward – for example, the B10L was the full low-floor 10-litre bus model, and the B10BLE was the low-entry equivalent.

Following the relative success of the front-engined double-deck Ailsa, developed by a Scottish Volvo dealer and later adopted by Volvo, there was a period when certain Volvo models were built and assembled in Scotland at Irvine, including the B6 midi, the mid-engined B10M and the Olympian double-decker. The success of the original Dennis Dart had prompted Volvo to create the B6, but although Volvo beat Dennis to the starting line with its low-floor B6LE version, the Dart SLF went on to outsell the Volvo equivalents.

This 1994 40-seat two-door Säffle-bodied Volvo B10L was demonstrated to potential buyers when it was new, and it is seen in Edinburgh in 1996, working with Lothian. Production versions of this style of body were built by Alexander (Belfast) and marketed as the Ultra. (Robert McGillivray)

A 1995 B6BLE with 36-seat Wright Crusader body is working for First Mainline in Sheffield in 1998, with lowkey EasiAccess branding.

In the Stagecoach hometown of Perth in 1997, a 1996 B6LE with Alexander ALX200 36-seat body is proudly proclaiming its low-floor credentials.

Delivered to National Express Dundee in 1997, a B10L with Wright Liberator 43-seat body is in Dundee in 2007.

A 1998 Huntingdon & District B10BLE with 47-seat Wright Renown body is in Cambridge in 2004.

This image shows a 1998 Go Wear Buses B10BLE with Wright Renown 44-seat body, promoting easy access for everyone at Washington Galleries bus station.

Starting its journey from Bradford Interchange, this 1999 Keighley & District B10BLE with Wright Renown 47-seat body is on the 662 Airedale Shuttle route.

Volvo worked hard to persuade UK customers to buy its articulated chassis, and First placed examples in several of its fleets. This is a 1999 B10LA with 55-seat Wright Fusion body working for First in Manchester in 2002.

A First Aberdeen 2000-delivered B10BLE with Alexander ALX300 44-seat body in Aberdeen in 2008.

In 2001, First London borrowed this new B7LA with Wright Eclipse Fusion 56-seat two-door body from First Hampshire and painted it red, in order to test the suitability of artics in London service.

FirstGroup was a major customer for the B7L. This is a 2001 Rider York example in York in 2007, with a Wright Eclipse Metro 41-seat body.

Optare

Ownership of the UK bus manufacturing industry has changed greatly over the past 40 years. The rationalisation at Leyland in the 1980s led to the closure of its Roe coachworks in Leeds in 1984, which in turn led to the creation of Optare in 1985, a company that majored in design and technical innovation. It survived a series of mergers and acquisitions involving United Bus, Optare's management, North American Bus Industries, the Darwen Group and Ashok Leyland, and in 2020, Optare was renamed Switch Mobility, as the electric vehicle arm of Ashok Leyland.

Optare's first single-deckers were step-entrance types built on proprietary chassis, but cleverly marketed as Optare models, so they were often best remembered by the Optare name: there was the Delta on DAF SB220; the Vecta on MAN 11.180/11.190; the Sigma on Dennis Lance; and the Prisma on Mercedes-Benz O405.

Then came the Optare integrals: the full-size Excel in 1995, and the Solo midibus in 1997. Both sold well, but the Solo was Optare's greatest success – a complete rethinking of the midibus concept that went on to sell more than 5,000 in its original and later SR forms.

Left: The Optare Excel was available between 1996 and 2004 in a variety of lengths ranging from 9.6m to 11.5m. This 11.5m 40-seater was supplied to Hutchison of Overtown in 1997, and it is seen in Wishaw in 2006, promoting the fact that it was a 'Buggy Bus' – although the 'Live Music, DJs, Dance' advertised on the cantrail panels related to a local club rather than additional on-board attractions.

Below: A 2000-delivered 10.7m Excel 39-seater operating with Safeguard of Guildford in 2019. (Keith McGillivray)

The hugely successful Solo was originally available in two lengths (8.5m and 9.2m), but the range of options, and the buses, subsequently lengthened with versions ranging from 7.1m to 10.2m. This 8.5m Solo is working for Stagecoach in 2010, leaving Preston's iconic bus station. It was new to Preston Bus in 2002.

Two Solos from the fleet of Coastal Coaches of Warton, in Lytham in 2013. They are 8.8m 28-seaters dating from 2009 and 2011.

The smallest Solos were 7.1m long, like this 22-seat 2011 delivery to Heyfordian of Bicester, seen in Oxford in 2012.

Leaving Dumfries in 2011, a new Stagecoach Western 8.8m Solo 27-seater on a Dumfries and Galloway tendered service, hence the livery.

DFL/VDL

The Dutch builder DAF first competed in the UK market in 1975 with mid-engined coach chassis, and its first bus model was the step-entrance SB220 in 1988, initially with Optare Delta bodywork. From 1997, a low-floor version of the SB220 was available, and this was bodied by Alexander, East Lancs, Ikarus and Northern Counties/Plaxton. A major customer for DAF, and later VDL, chassis was Arriva, supplied through the associated Arriva Bus & Coach dealership.

DAF Bus passed into the Dutch VDL Groep in 1993, and its products were rebranded as VDL in 2003. VDL also brought together other Dutch and Belgian bus builders Berkhof, Bova, Hainje and Jonckheere.

DAF/VDL moved to lighter-weight models from 2000 with the midi-size SB120 and SB180, and the full-size SB200. The SB120 and SB200 proved to be the most popular chassis, with sales of more than 700 SB120s and more than 800 SB200s – many, unsurprisingly, to Arriva companies.

Right: The full-size DAF SB220 chassis was introduced in low-entry form in 1997, and some early low-floor SB220s carried this style of body, the Northern Counties Paladin LF, a design subsequently adopted by Plaxton as the Prestige (some of the Northern Counties orders were completed by Plaxton). This 1997 Go North East example started life with Speedlink and is shown in Chester-le-Street in 2008.

Below: Arriva, which was also the importer of DAF and VDL models, inevitably bought large quantities of successive models for its UK fleets. This is an SB220 with Northern Counties Paladin LF bodywork, a 38-seat example that was new into Arriva's London fleet in 1998 and transferred to the North West & Wales fleet the following year. It is seen in 2012 in Liverpool.

Although most Arriva DAF and VDL types carry Wright bodies, a few carry Ikarus Citibus bodies, like this 44-seat Arriva Yorkshire SB200 in Leeds in 2007. New in 2002 to Aztecbird of Guiseley, it was bought by Arriva two years later.

DAF introduced its SB120 model in 2000 as a response to the successful Dennis Dart SLF. Arriva's London fleet received DAF SB120s with Wright Cadet bodies. This is a 9.4m 2003 two-door 26-seater in Croydon in 2016.

When this 2006 Arriva Cymru VDL SB120/Wright Cadet 39-seater was photographed picking up passengers at Bangor bus station in 2013, the DAF Bus name had given way to VDL Bus.

This is an Arriva Midlands 2007 SB120 with Wright Cadet 39-seat body, in Shrewsbury in 2013.

Go-Ahead Group's Go North East company was another customer for DAF and VDL chassis. This 2004 SB120 with Wright Cadet 39-seat body is seen in Newcastle in 2008.

Smaller, independent operators have also selected the SB120. In Crieff, in 2008, we see a Crieff Travel 2007 example with Plaxton Centro 40-seat body.

Above: Picking up passengers in Southampton in 2008 is a 2007 SB120 with Wright 39-seat body, from Go-Ahead's Bluestar fleet.

Right: An Arriva Durham County 2009 SB200 with Wright Commander 44-seat body pulls out of Durham bus station in 2016.

In Southport in 2015, an Arriva Merseyside SB200 with Wright Commander 44-seat body, new in 2010.

Mercedes-Benz

The legendary German giant Mercedes-Benz has been supplying vehicles to UK operators since the late 1960s – first coaches, then large numbers of minibuses from the 1980s and full-size service buses from the 1990s, the first of which was the step-entrance O405 from 1993. This was followed by the low-floor O405N, with West Midlands as the main customer, taking the complete Mercedes-Benz product while other operators specified Optare or Wright bodies. There were also a small number of articulated O405GNs.

From 2000, Mercedes-Benz supplied its Citaro model, first in O530 rigid form then as the articulated O530G, notably, and controversially, over 400 went to London operators, where concerns about cyclists' safety led to premature withdrawal of the Citaro fleet. Mercedes-Benz has sold more than 50,000 of successive Citaro models around the world.

Between 1998 and 2013, Mercedes-Benz sold nearly 1,500 O405 and Citaro models to UK operators.

Left: Travel West Midlands built up a fleet of rigid and articulated Mercedes-Benz buses. This is one of nearly 200 O405N 43-seaters delivered in 1998–99, seen in Birmingham in 1999.

Below: Between 2002 and 2008, London operators took delivery of over 400 Citaro O530G 49-seat three-door artics. This Stagecoach Selkent 2003 example passes through Trafalgar Square in 2008 with a London Central O530G in pursuit.

Above: A 2006 delivery into the Arriva Southern Counties fleet, this image shows a 39-seat Mercedes-Benz Citaro O530 at West Byfleet in 2008, liveried, appropriately, for Mercedes-Benz World at nearby Brooklands, served by the 436 route.

Right: Photographed leaving Oxford train station in 2012 is a 2008 Oxford Bus Citaro O530 40-seater heading for Abingdon.

The Mercedes-Benz OC500LE was supplied as a chassis for other bodybuilders, and just 11 were supplied to UK operators, all with MCV eVolution bodies. This included three for Perryman's of Berwick-upon-Tweed in 2012, as seen in Galashiels in 2017.

MAN

MAN is a long-standing German manufacturer that first exported coaches to the UK in 1980 but had previously supplied five step-entrance SG192R artics to South Yorkshire PTE in 1978.

From 1998, it sold substantial quantities of its A69 and A66 bus chassis, many to companies in the Stagecoach group. The main MAN low-floor bus models were the midi-size A76 (12.xxx), the larger A66 (14.xxx) and the full-size A69 (18.xxx). The '12', '14' and '18' refer to the gross weight in tonnes. There was also the 11.xxx series, bodied as buses and coaches; in bus form, they received Marshall and Optare bodies.

Left: Stagecoach turned to MAN for the chassis for its first large orders for full-size low-floor single-deckers. This 18.240 model with Alexander ALX300 42-seat body was new in 1999 with Stagecoach Transit, and it is seen in 2000 in Stockton.

Below: Stagecoach also bought small batches of MAN 18.240s with East Lancs Kinetic 42-seat bodies in 2006–07. This 2007 example is in Perth in 2008.

Above: The London operator Metroline took MAN 12.240s with 10.4m MCV eVolution 26-seat two-door bodies in 2007. This one is at Hatton Cross, on the fringes of Heathrow Airport, in 2008.

Right: The Scottish independent MacEwan received this MAN NL273F with Wright Meridian 44-seat body in 2009. It is seen in Dumfries in 2011.

Later Stagecoach MAN deliveries specified the 18.220 model with AD Enviro300 46-seat bodies, like this newly delivered 2009 Stagecoach example in Oxford.

A 2010 MAN 14.240 with MCV eVolution two-door 28-seat body working for Dales & District in Richmond in 2017. (Robert McGillivray)

Plaxton

What was known in the UK as the Plaxton Primo was actually the Hungarian-built Enterprise Plasma, a 7.9m midibus completed and sold by Plaxton at Scarborough. Between 2004 and 2010, Plaxton supplied 174 to a range of UK operators.

The Enterprise EB01 7.9m minibus was built in Hungary and was completed by Plaxton, marketed as the Primo. This Lippen of Paisley 28-seat 2006 delivery is seen in its hometown in 2009.

Reays of Wigton took delivery of 14 Primos in 2010, and this one is in Carlisle in 2011.

Other low-floor types

In addition to the larger quantities of low-floor buses supplied by the major manufacturers, there were several companies that each supplied fewer than 100 to UK operators.

The **Marshall Minibus** was really a *midi*bus, built by coachbuilders Marshall, which had acquired the rights to several Bedford models after General Motors closed the Bedford Dunstable plant in 1986. One was the Bedford JJL, a promising step-entrance midibus, which morphed into the Marshall Minibus, but this model gained a reputation for unreliability. Just 52 were built between 1996 and 1998.

Other early low-floor models that enjoyed limited success were the **Irisbus Agora Line**, designed by Renault for the UK market and supplied in part-built form for completion by Optare. Just 23 went to UK operators between 2002 and 2007; the **BMC Falcon 1100**, a Turkish-built 11m low-entry bus, of which 41 were sold to UK operators between 2003 and 2007; the Hawk midibus and Condor citybus, also exported by BMC, which were were mainly supplied for use in local authority school and welfare fleets; and the **Temsa Avenue**, a Turkish-built 42-seat citybus, of which 42 examples were exported to the UK in 2010–11, all but one being for Arriva fleets. Furthermore, around this time, **King Long** became the first Chinese manufacturer to export buses and coaches into the UK. Most King Long deliveries have been coaches, but there have been examples of its 9m-long XMQ6900J for independent operators, and its XMQ6127J, mainly for Airparks.

The Marshall Mini was a brave attempt to produce an integral midibus, but, between 1996 and 1998 only 186 were built. There were just 16 of the Mk2 version featured in this promotional leaflet, all for First's Centrewest fleet. (Marshall)

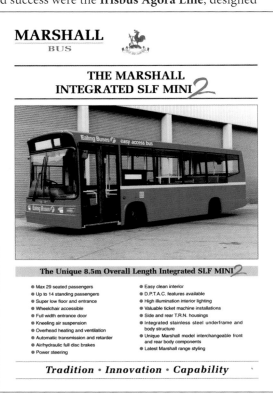

MARSHALL
BUS

THE MARSHALL INTEGRATED SLF MINI2

The Unique 8.5m Overall Length Integrated SLF MINI2

- Max 29 seated passengers
- Up to 14 standing passengers
- Super low floor and entrance
- Wheelchair accessible
- Full width entrance door
- Kneeling air suspension
- Overhead heating and ventilation
- Automatic transmission and retarder
- Air/hydraulic full disc brakes
- Power steering

- Easy clean interior
- D.P.T.A.C. features available
- High illumination interior lighting
- Valuable ticket machine installations
- Side and rear T.R.N. housings
- Integrated stainless steel underframe and body structure
- Unique Marshall model interchangeable front and rear body components
- Latest Marshall range styling

Tradition • Innovation • Capability

Chapter 6

The Second Generation

During the 1990s, UK bus operators gradually accepted that low-floor single-deckers were the way forward, but some were more cautious – or perhaps more price-conscious – and continued to buy step-entrance models. While the other large groups were enthusiastically embracing the new low-floor models, Stagecoach largely stuck to its tried and tested Volvo B10M/ Alexander PS step-entrance combination for its UK fleets outside London.

It had been evident from the start that there would be a premium to pay for low-floor models compared with their step-entrance predecessors. This could be 20 per cent for Dutch-built buses and more for German models. While this may not have been a problem on mainland Europe, it was certainly a cause for concern among UK operators. The availability of reliable chassis like the Dennis Dart helped UK bus companies to introduce fleets of low-floor single-deckers, and there seemed to be an awareness among the builders that wanted to export their models that the UK was a rather different market. Low-entry models with higher-set seating above and behind the rear axle were fine for most UK customers, although fully low-floor models designed for buses that often had centre and rear doors were bought as well. Although London contracts usually specified a second door for alighting passengers, most other operators were happy with a single front door. Fully low-floor models bought by UK operators included the Mercedes-Benz Citaro, Scania's N94 and OmniCity, and the Volvo B10L and B7L ranges.

The new century brought a series of new, improved models. Volvo's successful B7RLE appeared in 2003, and its successor, the B8RLE, was one of the last new diesel models to be introduced, taking to the streets in 2015. There was a rush of new models between 2005 and 2007, from Alexander Dennis, Optare and Scania, and then between 2010 and 2016 from Mercedes-Benz, Optare and Wright.

After the race that started in the 1990s to get cleaner, greener diesel-engined models on the market, the bus industry found itself in a new race: the race towards zero emissions. For most operators, this had started with a new breed of diesel-electric hybrids, followed by a rush towards battery-electrics, and biogas- and hydrogen-fuelled buses. And while the main players worked to meet these new demands, brand new manufacturers were springing up, hoping to cater for the important battery-electric market. As we shall see in the next chapter, most of the newcomers were developing single-deck city bus types, while the double-deck market tended to be in the hands of existing bus builders.

In the meantime, the major manufacturers were refining their existing ranges of low-floor single-deckers in the light of operator experience and the ever-tighter emissions standards. The UK market had settled down to five main players: importers Mercedes-Benz, Scania and Volvo, and two UK-based suppliers, Alexander Dennis and Wright. Alexander Dennis had largely switched to offering complete vehicles in the 2000s and Wright adopted a similar approach the following decade; both recognised that there was a shrinking demand for chassis and bodies from different manufacturers.

Volvo

The successful Volvo B10BLE was replaced in 2003 by the B7RLE, combining the front part of the B10BLE with the rear of its B7R coach chassis, providing a low-entry model that suited many UK operators. Over 2,000 were built between 2003 and 2014, the great majority with Wright Eclipse Urban bodies. Volvo admitted defeat for its midi-size range and stuck to full-size chassis after the last B6BLEs were delivered in 2002.

When the B7RLE was succeeded by the B8RLE in 2015, it was a time when orders for new diesel buses were slowing down. Many have bodies by MCV, which by this time was working closely with Volvo on new models.

Right: Volvo's first low-floor single-deck models for the UK market, the B7L, B10BLE and B10L, were replaced by the B7RLE, introduced in 2003. This 2004 Lothian Buses example with Wright Eclipse Urban 42-seat body is on a stretch of guided busway in 2005 that was later replaced by the new Edinburgh tramway.

Below: A 2005 43-seat B7RLE/Wright Eclipse Urban of Whitelaws of Stonehouse is seen in Hamilton in 2006.

An East Yorkshire 2006 43-seat B7RLE/Wright Eclipse Urban in Hull in 2011.

A 2006 Arriva Kent & Thameside B7RLE/Wright Eclipse Urban 40-seater on a stretch of bus-only road in 2007. It is on the Fastrack network, linking Dartford, Gravesend and Bluewater.

Wright built the revolutionary FTR StreetCar for FirstBus, based on a Volvo B7LA chassis. Note the tram-like appearance, with the driver isolated in a cab ahead of the front door. Just 38 were built in 2006–07, and most were used in North and West Yorkshire. This First West Yorkshire 2006 two-door 40-seater is in Leeds in 2013, operating on the 72 Hyperlink service linking Leeds with Bradford. (Keith McGillivray)

Wright-bodied buses are rare in the Stagecoach fleet, but this 2007 42-seat B7RLE/Wright Eclipse Urban, seen in Inverness in 2009, had been acquired from local operator, Rapson's, in 2008.

A National Express Dundee 2011 B7RLE with the facelifted Wright Eclipse Urban 2 style of body, in Dundee in 2012. It is named *Oor Wullie*, after the popular cartoon character 'born' in Dundee.

Left: Eclipse, the Gosport Fareham Rapid Bus Link, appropriately used Wright Eclipse Urban 2-bodied B7RLEs from First Hampshire & Dorset. This 2012 42-seater is seen in 2014.

Below: Between 2012 and 2014, a few late-model B7RLEs received bodies built by the Egyptian builder MCV. This 2014 B7RLE/MCV eVolution was in Skipton working with Kirkby Lonsdale Coach Hire on the Craven Connection route in 2018.

The B8RLE replaced the B7RLE in 2014, and as Wright was concentrating on building complete buses, Volvo turned to MCV as its body partner. This 2015 46-seat B8RLE/MCV eVolution is in Glasgow in 2022 with West Coast Motors.

Lothian Buses received MCV eVoRa 49-seat bodies on B8RLE chassis in 2021; this one is seen when new.

Optare

As we have seen, Optare survived changes of ownership and continued to produce attractive new complete integral vehicles. In 2005, the Tempo replaced the Excel, and like the Excel it was available in a range of length options – in this case between 10.6m and 12.6m.

This was followed in 2007 by the Versa, in essence a longer version of Optare's successful Solo model, which was itself upgraded as the Solo SR the same year. In 2013, Optare introduced the Metrocity, aimed at operators of London services and, as usual with Optare, offered it in various lengths, in this case between 9.9m and 11.5m. A battery electric version, the Metrocity EV, is covered in the next chapter.

Left: A London United 2008 Optare Versa V1040 two-door 27-seater on Kingston Bridge in 2016. The Optare type codes include the overall length, so a V1040 is a 10.4m long Versa, and an M960SR is a Solo 9.6m SR version.

Below: The updated Solo SR sold well, like this 2008 Preston Bus M960SR 32-seater in 2015.

A new Go North East Versa V1110 40-seater, branded for the 54 Saltwell Park route, passes Newcastle Central station in 2009.

London United bought 16 Tempo X1200 34-seat two-door 12m-long buses in 2011, and this one is in Hounslow in 2016.

This image shows an Arriva Southern Counties 37-seat 2011 Versa V1110 with revised frontal styling in Guildford in 2017.

A TrentBarton Tempo SR in Derby in 2014, with a restyled front-end treatment. A 41-seater, it was new in 2012.

TrentBarton again, and a 2014 Versa V1110 36-seater in Heanor's H1 livery leaves Derby for Heanor when new.

This is the prototype Metrocity, a 10.6m 29-seater built in 2013, and it is seen here operating with Quality Line in Kingston in 2017.

Alexander Dennis

The highly successful Dennis Dart morphed into the Enviro200 Dart under Alexander Dennis and continued the Dart's impressive sales success. Available in a range of lengths, the E200 Dart combined a chassis built by Dennis at Guildford with an Alexander body built at Falkirk or Scarborough. Small numbers of E200s were bodied by East Lancs, MCV and Optare, and the model also sold into export markets, notably New Zealand, where Alexander Dennis worked with Kiwi Bus Builders.

The E200 was upgraded in 2015 when the MMC (Major Model Change) version first appeared, and longer variants replaced the long-established Enviro300 as the Alexander Dennis' full-length home market model.

Left: The Alexander Dennis Enviro200 Dart quickly became the most popular single-deck type in London service. While the majority were complete Alexander Dennis buses, Go-Ahead London bought Optare-bodied E200 Darts that were unique in London service. This 2009 two-door 10.4m 29-seater is in Wimbledon in 2016.

Below: A short-length (8.9m) 28-seat E200 of First Glasgow in Motherwell, when new in 2009.

A 2010 Halton Transport E200 40-seater is pictured here against the imposing background of the Port of Liverpool building, one of the Three Graces that dominate Liverpool's Pier Head, in 2014.

A Stagecoach South Wales 2011 38-seat 10.8m E200 in Cardiff in 2013, wearing vinyls for the 26 Blackwood-Cardiff service.

At Elephant and Castle in 2016, a 2011 9.3m Go-Ahead London E200 two-door 24-seater sports the dark grey skirt panels that were permitted before the all-red livery rule came in.

The extra length of this 10.8m Glasgow Citybus 2012 E200 41-seater is evident in this 2019 view in central Glasgow.

Left: A 2012 Arriva London South 31-seat two-door 10.8m E200 in unrelieved red livery at Elmers End Interchange in 2013.

Below: In Christchurch in 2022, this 2012 Yellow Buses E200 10.8m 38-seater still carries a livery celebrating 50 years since the last Bournemouth trolleybus in 1969.

The restyled MMC (Major Model Change) version of the Enviro200 Dart appeared in 2015. A 2015 10.5m two-door 31-seat Stagecoach version is seen at Ilford Station in 2016.

Right: A 2015 delivery to the First Lanarkshire fleet, an 11.8m 41-seat E200MMC is in Glasgow in 2022, wearing the Lanarkshire Connect version of the First livery.

Below: The 11.8m length of this 2015 Stagecoach Fife E200MMC is clear in this 2016 shot at Dunfermline bus station. The longer versions replaced the long-standing Enviro300 that dated back to the difficult TransBus years.

London operators bought the E200MMC in substantial quantities. This 2016 Abellio 10.9m two-door 31-seater is at Elephant and Castle when new.

This 8.9m 31-seat E200MMC was delivered to Courtney of Bracknell in 2017. It is seen at Maidenhead in 2019, the year the Courtney business was acquired by Reading Buses; it now trades as Thames Valley Buses.

A recently delivered Borders Buses 39-seat E200 at the Tweedbank terminus awaits passengers from the Borders Railway in 2017.

Right: Go South Coast's More operation uses E200MMCs like this 2018 11.8m 38-seater, seen picking up passengers in Bournemouth in 2019.

Below: Falcon Buses of Byfleet runs routes in Surrey and into Kingston. This 9.0m 2018 E200MMC crossing Kingston Bridge in 2019 is a 30-seater.

Scania

As chassis-builders adapted their ranges to include engines that met the ever more stringent Euro regulations on emissions, Scania introduced new versions of its diesel chassis and complete buses. First was the integral CN230UB OmniCity in 2006, followed in 2007 by the CK230UB OmniLink, the chassis-only K230UB, and the Alexander Dennis-bodied K270UB gas buses for Reading and Stagecoach Busways. The type designations followed a similar pattern to those described in Chapter 5, although the series and engine capacity numbers have been replaced by output figures, 230hp, etc.

Left: A 2008 43-seat Brighton & Hove Scania CK230UB OmniLink, branded for the 50 route, in Brighton in 2009.

Below: Hallmark, part of the Rotala group, runs services on the fringes of London, and this 2011 Scania K230UB OmniLink 45-seater is leaving Kingston's Cromwell Road bus station in 2017.

In 2014, Stagecoach in Inverness was using this 2012 N230UB with Alexander Dennis Enviro300 43-seat bodywork on the Jet service linking the city with Inverness Airport.

Cardiff Bus bought Scania N94UA 53-seat artics in 2006, and this one is seen in 2018.

Wright

After its spectacular success when it broke into the British bodybuilding market in the 1990s, Wright turned to building complete buses, first with the hybrid electric Electrocity in 2005, then with the double-deck Gemini 2DL based on DAF running units from 2007, and then with the successful StreetLite from 2010. This has been followed by a range of innovative diesel, battery electric and hydrogen models.

Left: The Wright StreetLite was available in two main layouts – the more common DF (door forward) and the WF (wheel forward); this is a 10.8m WF 37-seater in 2013, operating for Preston Bus. This was the very first StreetLite built, in 2010.

Below: The only WF StreetLites in London service are operated by Go-Ahead. This 2012 8.8m 28-seater is seen in Ilford in 2016.

Above: In the Arriva Sapphire livery and branded for the 321 service linking Luton and Watford, a 2014 DF 41-seat model in Arriva's The Shires fleet is seen in St Albans in 2016.

Right: FirstBus has bought hundreds of StreetLites, and this 2015 First Midland Bluebird DF 11.5m 41-seater is in Edinburgh in 2022. It is branded for the Royal Route, linking Edinburgh with Linlithgow and Stirling.

A 31-seat 2016 StreetLite DF 10.8m from Go-Ahead's London fleet crosses Putney Bridge in 2017.

Mercedes-Benz

Before Mercedes-Benz introduced its upgraded integral Citaro O295 range in the UK in 2014, it sold 11 examples of its OC500LE chassis with MCV bodies, but the short-length O295K, and particularly the full-size O295, have sold in much greater number.

McGill's was an early customer for the restyled Mercedes-Benz O295 Citaro, with deliveries starting with a batch of 14 in 2014. This first delivery included this 41-seater, seen in Glasgow in 2022.

Blackpool Transport bought the O295 Citaro in 2015, in 39-seat form, as seen in Blackpool when new.

The only examples of the 10.6m Citaro O295K in London service were 28-seat two-door buses bought by the Epsom Coaches Group Quality Line fleet in 2016, as seen in Cromwell Road bus station in Kingston in 2017.

Cardiff Bus has invested in several batches of the Citaro model. This 2017 O295 41-seater is seen in 2018.

Chapter 7
The New Generation

Bus manufacturers may have thought that once they had found their way through the minefield of Euro emissions regulations, reaching Euro VI in 2013 would be the end of it. But in a world looking for every way to reduce carbon emissions, there were already experiments as manufacturers tried to second-guess what form the next generation of buses would take.

Electric and gas buses had been around in the early days of buses, and over the years manufacturers and operators built and operated experimental buses that often only served to highlight their impracticalities, particularly with heavy batteries on electric buses and problems with access to gas supplies. But with concerns about climate change, there have been renewed efforts to design and build practical new-generation types.

In the UK, these were often produced with London orders in mind, and the first three buses to appear were Mercedes-Benz Citaro hydrogen fuel-cell buses, which were delivered to First in 2003. The combination of hydrogen gas and oxygen generated electricity to drive these buses. These buses were succeeded by five fuel-cell Wright-bodied VDL SB200s. Van Hool supplied ten three-axle A330FC hydrogen single-deckers for use in Aberdeen by First and Stagecoach in 2014, and two hydrogen two-axle A330FCs to Tower Transit in 2017. In 2020, First Aberdeen placed the world's first hydrogen fuel-cell double-deckers, Wright Hydroliners, in service. Wright has also demonstrated a single-deck Hydroliner.

The next technology was the diesel-electric hybrid, combining a diesel engine and electric batteries. The first examples in the UK were Designline Olympus hybrids imported by Stagecoach from New Zealand for QuayLink routes in Newcastle in 2004–2005, followed quickly by Wright Electrocity hybrids in London in 2005. Double-deck hybrids followed between 2007 and 2020, and these have easily outnumbered single-deck versions. Optare introduced Tempo hybrids in 2008 and Versa hybrids in 2010, and Alexander Dennis produced a small batch of Enviro200 hybrids in 2009, followed by larger E350H models from 2012. Volvo supplied many hybrid double-deckers to UK operators, but only small batches of its single-deck 7900 hybrid.

Meanwhile, gas buses were still on the menu. Buses running on compressed natural gas (CNG) have surfaced from time to time, but never really made their mark in the UK. More recently, biogas, renewable natural gas, was being pushed by Scania, which sold single-deck and double-deck models into a mix of municipal, FirstGroup, and independent fleets from 2013.

But the greatest potential seems to have been found in all-electric buses, and the race was on to get single-deck and double-deck types into major fleets. London General introduced two Chinese-built BYD K9E all-electric single-deckers in 2013, and BYD supplied its first double-deckers in 2016. From that time, new electric models appeared on the UK streets from Caetano, Irizar, Switch and Yutong, and there were substantial deliveries of BYD/AD single-deckers and double-deckers, with electric models in the pipeline from Mercedes-Benz, Scania and Volvo, as well as from new names eager to break into the market, like Arrival, Higer, and established UK builder Mellor with its Sigma range. Alexander Dennis has announced that it is developing a new small bus and a new electric double-deck, both in-house products that will complement the successful BYD/AD range.

Bus builders that have been building increasingly refined single-deckers for decades have had to embrace the new technology, particularly as the market is proving attractive to a new raft of manufacturers. And it would be wrong for the established names to be complacent, remembering that they too started small and may have been written off as cheeky upstarts by the dominant manufacturers of the time, many of which have fallen by the wayside in the past 50 years.

The signs are that electric buses will dominate orders in the years to come, but hydrogen buses, after a couple of early attempts, returned with single-deck Van Hool types for service in Aberdeen and the world's first hydrogen double-deckers, also for Aberdeen. Like all new buses built for UK service since 2000, the diesel-electric hybrids, hydrogen and battery-electric buses shown here have all been of low-floor layout.

Hybrids

Right: The first serious attempts in the new century to break away from reliance on fossil fuels used hybrid diesel-electric buses. Stagecoach set the ball rolling by importing ten Designline Olymbus hybrids from New Zealand in 2005. The two-door 29-seaters operated the Quaylink services in Newcastle, as seen here in 2008.

Below: The first hybrid diesel-electric single-deckers in London were six 10.2m Wright Electrocity 26-seaters delivered to Go-Ahead's London Central fleet in 2005–2006. This one is seen at Elephant and Castle 11 years later.

London United bought five 29-seat two-door hybrid Alexander Dennis 10.2m E200H Darts in 2009. This one is seen in Kingston in 2016, with the slogan 'Another red bus going green for London'. Double-deck hybrids had been in London fleets since 2006 and would go on to greatly outnumber their single-deck equivalents in London and the rest of the UK.

Optare Versa V790H hybrids were used on the free Metro Shuttle service in Manchester. Two 7.9m 28-seaters, new in 2010, are seen at Manchester Piccadilly station in 2011.

Henderson Travel of Hamilton was using this newly delivered hybrid 37-seat Alexander Dennis E200H on a Strathclyde Partnership for Transport-contracted service when photographed in Airdrie in 2011.

In service in Aberdeen in 2014, this 2012 Stagecoach Bluebird Buses AD E350H 41-seat hybrid is wearing a green version of what was then Stagecoach's corporate livery.

Volvo's single-deck hybrid model was the 7900H. This is a 40-seat 2013 delivery for First Essex Buses at Basildon, pictured when new. (Keith McGillivray)

Wright produced a hybrid version of its StreetLite DF model, and this 2014 Arriva Northumbria 44-seater is seen in Newcastle in 2017.

Gas

MAN and Scania have supplied gas buses to UK operators, mainly in the local authority sector. This MAN NL273F EcoCity with 41-seat Caetano body was built as a demonstrator in 2011 and is seen working with Lothian Buses in 2012.

Reading Buses has been a strong advocate of gas buses, and this 37-seat Optare Solo M1020 started life with Stagecoach in Lincoln in 2006 and was acquired by Reading for conversion to compressed natural gas (CNG). It is pictured in 2017.

In addition to a fleet of CNG double-deckers, Reading Buses has Scania K270UB gas buses with Alexander Dennis 42-seat bodies. This one is seen in 2013 when new.

Electric

Over the years, there have been several experiments with battery electric buses. This is Selnec's Seddon/Chloride Silent Rider, charging in Manchester in 1974, a 41-seater based on a Seddon Pennine RU.

Go-Ahead's London Central fleet received two of these 12m-long BYD K9E two-door battery-electric 21-seaters in 2013, and this one is at Waterloo in 2014.

First York bought 12 Optare Versa V1110EV models for the York Park & Ride services in 2014–2015. This newly delivered example is passing under the city walls in 2015.

London operators started to buy BYD electric buses with Alexander Dennis bodies in 2016. This is a 31-seat 2018 Metroline D8UR example at King's Cross in 2019, with St Pancras station as a backdrop.

Left: Yutong electric buses have become popular with operators around the UK. This Go North East 2020 Yutong E12 35-seater is seen in Newcastle in 2021. (Keith McGillivray)

Below: Cardiff Bus has also bought Yutong E12s, like this 2021 37-seater photographed in 2022. It wears a retro livery celebrating 120 years of municipal Transport in the Welsh capital. (Sholto Thomas)

Above: Stagecoach bought six Volvo 7900EV 40-seaters for its Western Buses operation, based in Kilmarnock. This 2021 delivery is seen in the East Ayrshire village of Priestland in 2022. (Keith McGillivray)

Right: A route-branded 2021 First Glasgow BYD D9UR with AD 40-seat body is seen in Glasgow in 2022.

Below: This 2022 delivery to Newport Bus, a Yutong E10 33-seater is at the ITT Hub event at Farnborough when new. (Keith McGillivray)

Mellor, a long-established UK builder of bodies for minibuses and midibuses, announced its battery-electric Sigma range in 2021, which will include 7m, 8m, 9m, 10m, 11m and 12m models. This detail from a 2022 advert shows the family resemblance across the range, with 7m, 8m and 10m variants represented.

Hydrogen

Eight of these hydrogen VDL SB200s with Wright 34-seat bodies were delivered to the First Capital fleet in 2010 for the RV1 route, which links Covent Garden and Tower Gateway. This one is seen in 2018.

In 2014, Van Hool supplied ten of these three-axle A330FC hydrogen-powered 42-seaters for services in Aberdeen. Six went into the Stagecoach Bluebird Buses fleet, like this bus, seen in 2019. (Keith McGillivray)

Right: Tower Transit received two of these hydrogen Van Hool A330FC two-door 33-seaters in 2017, as seen at the Covent Garden terminus of the RV1 route in 2018. (Keith McGillivray)

Below: Built by Caetano as a demonstrator in 2020, a hydrogen H2.City Gold 33-seat two-door model, at the ITT Hub event at Farnborough in 2022. (Keith McGillivray)

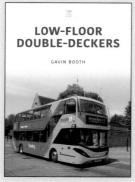
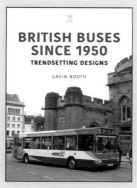
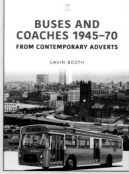
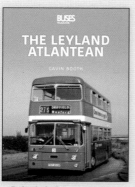
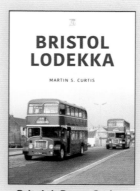
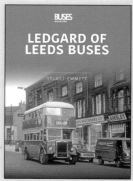